Mean Machines

Customized Cars

Kane Miller
A DIVISION OF EDC PUBLISHING

Kane Miller Books, A Division of EDC Publishing
First American Edition 2015

Created and produced by Green Android Ltd
www.greenandroid.co.uk
Copyright © Green Android Ltd 2014

Images by kind permission:
Front cover main image and page 28–29 Five Axis, Troy Sumitomo
Liberty Walk
Bulletproof Automotive
Jordi Miranda
Fesler Productions
Daimler AG
Group Lotus plc
Mansory Design and Holding, GmbH
Startech by CRD
G–Power, Germany
Romeo Ferraris, Italy
Honda Motor Europe Ltd
Bentley Motors
Edo Competition Motorsport, GmbH

For information contact:
Kane Miller, A Division of EDC Publishing
P.O. Box 470663
Tulsa, OK 74147-0663
www.kanemiller.com
www.edcpub.com
www. usbornebooksandmore.com

Library of Congress Control Number: 2014958064

Paperback ISBN: 978-1-61067-419-5
Hardcover ISBN: 978-1-61067-429-4

Printed and bound in China

Contents

See page 32 for a glossary of technical words.

Lamborghini *Murciélago*

Japanese tuning **experts** Liberty Walk have created a unique custom kit for the exceptional **Lamborghini** Murciélago. Named the "LB–R Zero Fighter," the kit's **military** design has been inspired by the Zero Fighter planes that were used during **World War II**. The kit includes eye-catching matte-green **paintwork** and some superb-looking **camouflage** lips on the new Werfen GT–04 wheels. Driving this outstanding customized **supercar** will get the driver a lot of attention.

Heated side mirrors

Aluminum alloy wheels

Rear spoiler

9.6-inch-wide front tires

Camouflage-patterned wheel lips

Side splitter

13.2-inch-wide rear tires

Air inlet

Scissor doors

Front splitter

LED taillights

Cooling vent

Central exhaust system

Rear diffuser

Measurements	
Length	181.5 in
Width	80.5 in
Height	44.7 in
Weight	3671 lb

Top speed	**211** mph
0–60 mph	**3.3** seconds
Power	**640** horsepower

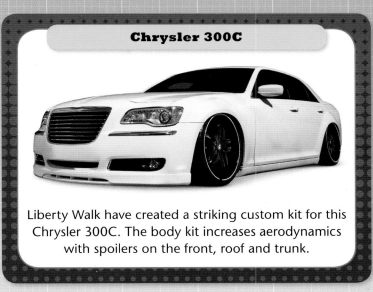

Chrysler 300C

Liberty Walk have created a striking custom kit for this Chrysler 300C. The body kit increases aerodynamics with spoilers on the front, roof and trunk.

Above Inside the cabin of the car the military theme is continued. The seats are covered in special camouflage-themed fabric.

Right The LB-R Zero Fighter has been fitted with a nitrous oxide injector for the times when a driver requires an extra burst of acceleration.

Below The cool camouflage trim is found throughout the car. It appears on the lower door molding bearing the famous Murciélago name.

Scion FR-S Concept One

Bulletproof Automotive set out to **transform** a standard Scion FR-S into a high-**performing** custom car that will rival the fastest supercars. The engine has been heavily modified with an upgraded **turbocharger** and a new exhaust system. The exterior has been **customized** to be aerodynamic and **lightweight**. The roof, wings and trunk have all been replaced in lightweight carbon fiber. This **stunning** car is finally treated to an authentic **Lamborghini** Balloon White full paint conversion.

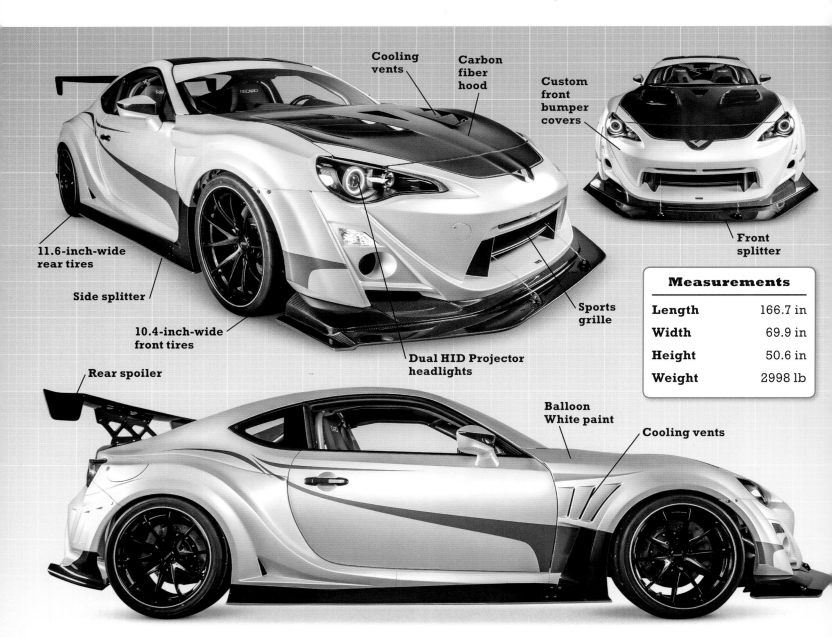

Cooling vents

Carbon fiber hood

Custom front bumper covers

Front splitter

11.6-inch-wide rear tires

Side splitter

10.4-inch-wide front tires

Sports grille

Dual HID Projector headlights

Rear spoiler

Balloon White paint

Cooling vents

Measurements	
Length	166.7 in
Width	69.9 in
Height	50.6 in
Weight	2998 lb

Nissan GT-R

This GT–R has been customized to balance technology with history and beauty. Aerodynamics are kept functional, while the wheels exude luxury and quality.

Above Bulletproof have used luxurious gloss-coated carbon fiber on the custom dashboard, steering wheel and gear shifter.

Right Inside the cabin are the two Recaro RS-G bucket seats, which have been upholstered using a bright-red Alcantara material.

Above Thanks to the modified turbocharged engine, Bulletproof's Concept One produces an outstanding 500 hp.

Aston Martin DBS

Specialist tuners Anderson Germany have **customized** the Aston Martin DBS to create the Casino Royale, as a **tribute** to the James Bond film that featured a DBS. **Power** has been increased with the addition of a new **lightweight** exhaust system with catalytic converters and a fine-tuned ECU. The stunning matte-gray paintwork **contrasts** with several **semigloss** gray accents throughout the body. The car has been given a cool set of black five-spoke wheels with bronze-colored brake **calipers**.

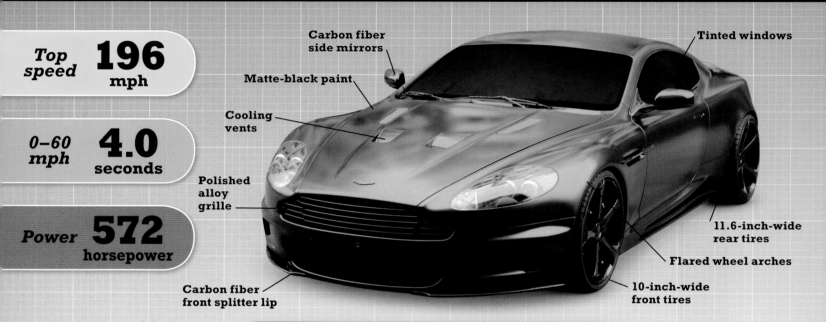

Top speed **196** mph

0–60 mph **4.0** seconds

Power **572** horsepower

Carbon fiber side mirrors

Matte-black paint

Cooling vents

Polished alloy grille

Carbon fiber front splitter lip

Tinted windows

11.6-inch-wide rear tires

Flared wheel arches

10-inch-wide front tires

Below Many of the interior elements, such as the newly updated center console, have been made in a lightweight carbon fiber material.

Measurements	
Length	185.9 in
Width	75.0 in
Height	50.4 in
Weight	3737 lb

Left The upholstery is black leather-effect carbon fiber with Alcantara, along with orange seams to give an elegant and unique look.

Volkswagen

The Volkswagen Polo GTI 6R **Synergetic Effects** is the result of **collaboration** between a number of styling and tuning companies. The whole car has been **foiled** in a dramatic pink camouflage design produced by CFC StylingStation. The car's chassis has been **stiffened** and **modified** to improve the driving experience. The interior boasts an awe-inspiring acoustic system, with .75-inch silk **tweeters** and an 8-inch active **subwoofer**. This one-of-a-kind Polo will turn heads wherever it goes.

Right The car is equipped with the most exquisite combination of bold-pink wheel rims and high-performance Falken tires.

Measurements

Length	155.6 in
Width	66.2 in
Height	57.2 in
Weight	2798 lb

Above For added drama the car has been modified with some bespoke carbon fiber parts such as the wing mirror covers and rear bumper.

Panoramic sunroof

Carbon fiber wing mirror cover

Camouflage design foil wrap

Custom-painted wheels

8.5-inch-wide rear tires

8.5-inch-wide front tires

Top speed **142** mph

0–60 mph **6.9** seconds

Power **180** horsepower

Buick

Lucerne CXS

This Buick Lucerne CXS has been customized by the **American** Fesler Built company. To create this sleek, **elegant** car, Fesler painted the bodywork and wheels in a bold red. A new sports **suspension** and MagnaFlow exhaust systems have been fitted, while the **high-performance** tires and **custom-built** brakes provide an exciting drive. Inside the cabin you will find **state-of-the-art** technology including two DVD headrest monitors with wireless headphones and a **navigation** system.

Measurements	
Length	203.2 in
Width	73.8 in
Height	58.0 in
Weight	3763 lb

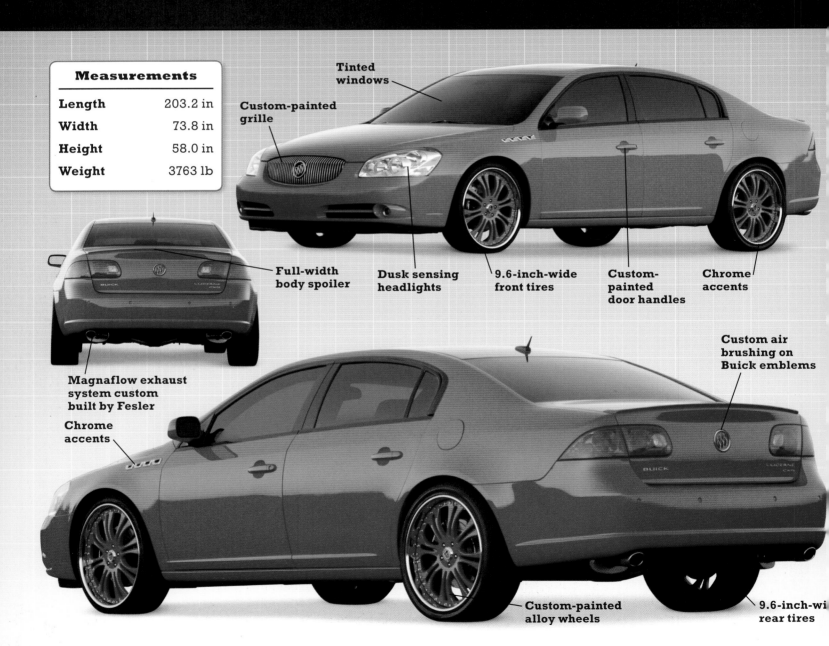

Tinted windows

Custom-painted grille

Full-width body spoiler

Dusk sensing headlights

9.6-inch-wide front tires

Custom-painted door handles

Chrome accents

Magnaflow exhaust system custom built by Fesler

Chrome accents

Custom air brushing on Buick emblems

Custom-painted alloy wheels

9.6-inch-wi rear tires

Top speed	**131** mph
0–60 mph	**6.9** seconds
Power	**275** horsepower

Right The interior luxurious feel is created by the use of high-quality black leather with red suede accents that match the car's paintwork.

Below The cabin boasts modifications, including the trim painted to match the interior and an in-dash DVD and navigation unit.

Buick Riviera

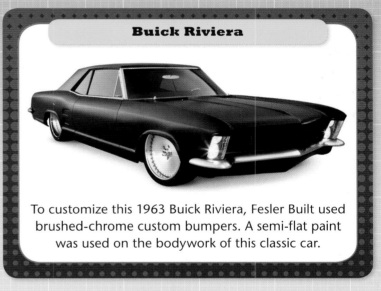

To customize this 1963 Buick Riviera, Fesler Built used brushed-chrome custom bumpers. A semi-flat paint was used on the bodywork of this classic car.

Above Fesler Built pride themselves on their attention to detail and this can be seen in the way that the unique monotone color theme has even been used on the engine.

Mercedes SLS AMG GT3

To celebrate its 45th birthday, AMG have built a special **racing** version of the Mercedes SLS called the SLS AMG GT3. The **bodywork** has been given a unique **graphite**-matte finish, as have the stunning 12–spoke wheels. The main differences between this **dynamic** race version and the standard SLS are the improved aerodynamics and the **lightweight** body. There have only been five of these **incredible** cars built, making them some of the most **desirable** driving machines in the world today.

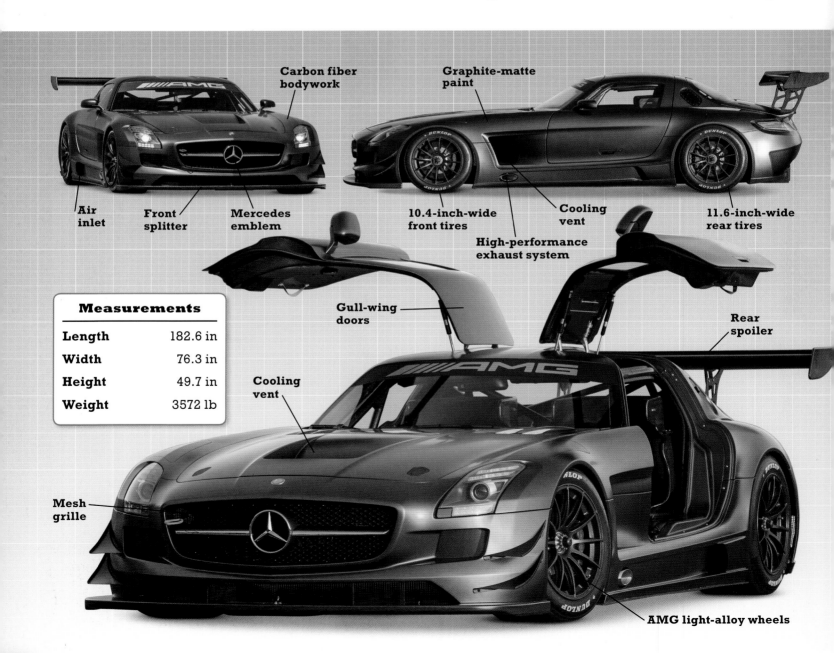

Carbon fiber bodywork

Graphite-matte paint

Air inlet

Front splitter

Mercedes emblem

10.4-inch-wide front tires

Cooling vent

High-performance exhaust system

11.6-inch-wide rear tires

Gull-wing doors

Rear spoiler

Measurements	
Length	182.6 in
Width	76.3 in
Height	49.7 in
Weight	3572 lb

Cooling vent

Mesh grille

AMG light-alloy wheels

Top speed	**199** mph
0–60 mph	**3.7** seconds
Power	**600** horsepower

Mercedes-AMG team

The SLS AMG GT3 has enjoyed tremendous success in motor sports. In its debut year, teams driving the SLS AMG GT3 won 26 races on three continents.

Above Inside are some more special touches. The roll cage paint matches the exterior and the dashboard is given a matte carbon fiber look.

Right The 6.2-liter V8 engine has been tuned to produce outstanding speeds and significant higher power than the road-going version.

Below The finishing touch that proves this car is something very special is the "1 of 5" emblem which can be found on the seat headrests.

Lotus *Exige V6 Cup R*

The Exige V6 Cup R is the **racing** version of the Exige V6 Cup. The car has a **customized** specification including a higher downforce, improved aerodynamics, a weight reduction and an increase to the power **output**. This **aggressive-looking** machine boasts competition-spec suspension, plumbed-in fire extinguisher, variable **traction** control, track-focused Pirelli tires and upgraded brakes. This **powerful** machine not only looks stunning, but gives a **dazzling** performance on the racetrack.

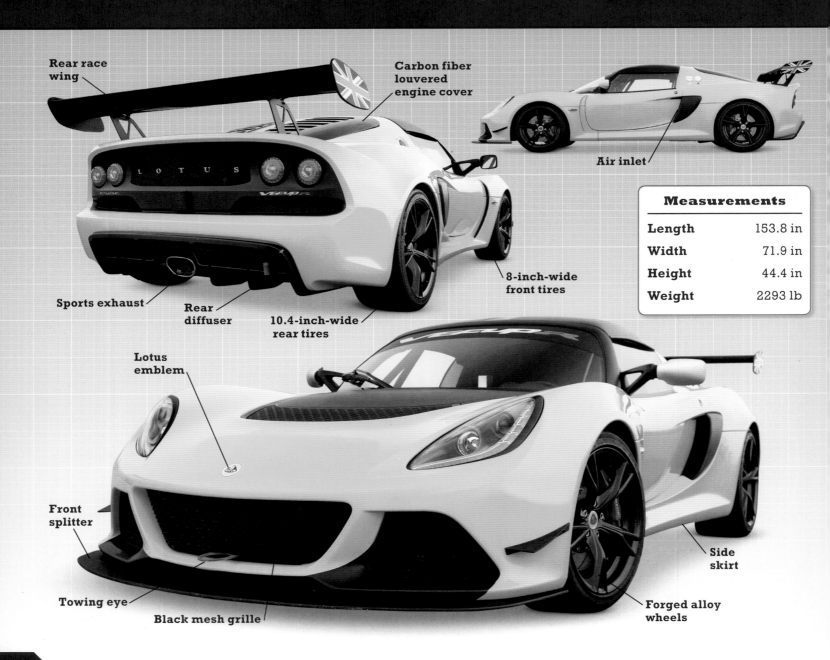

Rear race wing

Carbon fiber louvered engine cover

Air inlet

Sports exhaust

Rear diffuser

10.4-inch-wide rear tires

8-inch-wide front tires

Lotus emblem

Front splitter

Towing eye

Black mesh grille

Side skirt

Forged alloy wheels

Measurements	
Length	153.8 in
Width	71.9 in
Height	44.4 in
Weight	2293 lb

Top speed	170+ mph
0–60 mph	3.7 seconds
Power	366 horsepower

Left The Cup R has a super lightweight carbon fiber driver's seat with full racing harness and an incredibly strong roll cage.

Below Inside you will find an almost completely bare interior. It has been stripped of all nonessentials, to keep weight as low as possible.

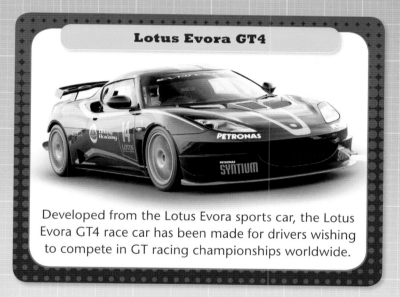

Lotus Evora GT4

Developed from the Lotus Evora sports car, the Lotus Evora GT4 race car has been made for drivers wishing to compete in GT racing championships worldwide.

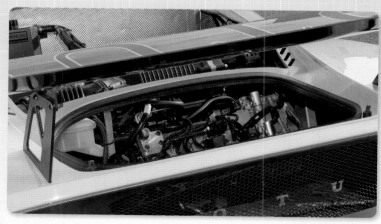

Above Lotus have used a 3.5-liter V6 Toyota engine that comes equipped with a powerful supercharger. This helps to improve the acceleration and top speed of this impressive car.

Bugatti *Veyron*

German company **Mansory**, who specialize in creating exclusive luxury cars, have taken the Bugatti Veyron and created a **spectacular** vehicle. This **outstanding** machine has new front fascia with different wings, shorter hood and a redesigned apron. Almost all the **bodywork** components are made from **lightweight**, strong carbon fiber. The car also comes with **v-shaped** LED daytime running lights as well as **modified** side skirts, together with bigger air inlets on the flanks.

Above This amazing car boasts many beautiful details, such as the Vivere name embedded onto the carbon fiber fuel cap.

Left The luxurious interior benefits from LED ambient lighting, a leather-wrapped steering wheel and carbon fiber applications.

Measurements	
Length	175.7 in
Width	78.7 in
Height	45.6 in
Weight	4162 lb

Top speed **252** mph

0–60 mph **2.7** seconds

Power **1001** horsepower

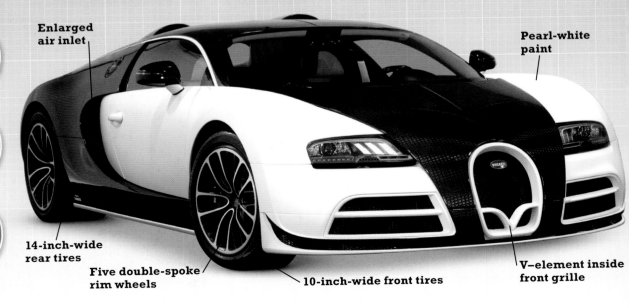

Enlarged air inlet

Pearl-white paint

14-inch-wide rear tires

Five double-spoke rim wheels

10-inch-wide front tires

V–element inside front grille

Tesla *Roadster Sport*

Specialist tuning company Brabus have taken the **exciting** Tesla Roadster Sport and customized it. The **electric-powered** car has an **aerodynamic** body kit, some customized lights, new wheels and alterations to the interior. The most **innovative** modification is the space sound **generator**, which pipes a choice of traditional engine noises into the cabin of this quiet electric car. The settings include a typical **V8**, race car engine and two **futuristic** soundscapes named beam and warp.

Matte-white paint

Carbon fiber rear diffuser

Alloy wheels

LED daytime running lights

Air inlet

8.5-inch-wide front tires

Cooling vent

10-inch-wide rear tires

Top speed	**125** mph
0–60 mph	**3.7** seconds
Power	**302** horsepower

Measurements	
Length	155.4 in
Width	73.7 in
Height	44.4 in
Weight	2723 lb

Below Even charging the battery on this electric Roadster looks cool, with its illuminated charge port underneath the cap.

Right The cabin features white seams to reflect the exterior color. The floor is upholstered with lightweight leather for added exclusivity.

BMW *M3 GT2 R*

G–POWER have used their tuning experience to **customize** a BMW M3 GT2 R into the **hottest** road-legal M3 around. They have created a modified aerodynamic package made entirely from **lightweight** carbon fiber to help increase **downforce** and save some weight. The addition of a **supercharger** to the powerful engine, a tailor-made cooling system and ceramic brakes increase performance. A **titanium** exhaust system gives a deep throaty **growl** that will turn heads whenever it is driven.

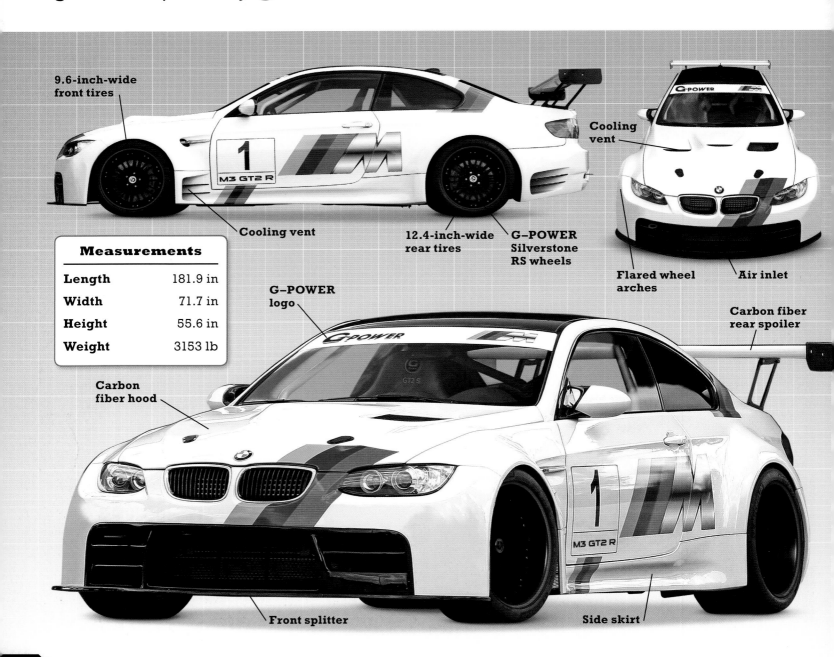

9.6-inch-wide front tires

Cooling vent

Cooling vent

12.4-inch-wide rear tires

G–POWER Silverstone RS wheels

Flared wheel arches

Air inlet

Carbon fiber rear spoiler

G–POWER logo

Carbon fiber hood

Front splitter

Side skirt

Measurements	
Length	181.9 in
Width	71.7 in
Height	55.6 in
Weight	3153 lb

Top speed **206** mph

0–60 mph **3.6** seconds

Power **720** horsepower

Right For the interior, G–POWER have installed carbon fiber racing front bucket seats and taken away the rear seats to save weight.

Below The fabrics inside this exciting M3 GT2 R feature numerous leather and Alcantara elements with blue contrast stitching.

BMW M3 GTS

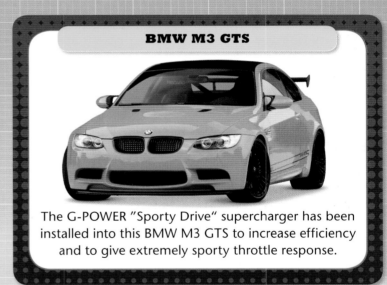

The G-POWER "Sporty Drive" supercharger has been installed into this BMW M3 GTS to increase efficiency and to give extremely sporty throttle response.

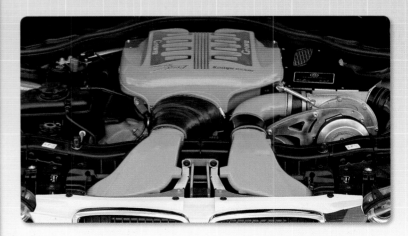

Above To achieve the mind-blowing 720 horsepower output a G–POWER M3 "Sporty Drive" supercharger has been added together with a specially designed new cooling system.

Abarth 500 Cinquone Stradale

This 500 Abarth has been given an extraordinary **overhaul** by Romeo Ferraris to become the **outstanding** 500 Cinquone Stradale. The new **aerodynamic** body kit includes front and rear enlargements to increase the width of the car by 2 inches on each side. The **1.4-liter** engine has been improved and updated with the **installation** of a powered turbine, special pistons, new **camshafts** and a double-outlet exhaust. This car not only has **sensational** looks, but also offers dazzling performance.

Abarth emblem

Full-width rear spoiler

Enlarged grille and air inlet

8.5-inch-wide front tires

Enlarged side skirts

8.5-inch-wide rear tires

Carbon fiber rear diffuser

Central exhaust system

New hood with cooling vents

Enlarged front bumper

Front fog lights

Front splitter

Enlarged wheel arches

Measurements	
Length	145.7 in
Width	68.9 in
Height	57.0 in
Weight	2359 lb

Top speed **157** mph

0–60 mph **5.5** seconds

Power **300** horsepower

Left Inside this small car's cabin you will find the driver's and passenger's racing bucket seats and four-point red harnesses.

Below The carbon fiber dashboard made by Romeo Ferraris, together with the Alcantara and leather interior fabrics create a stylish cabin.

500 Corsa Cinquone

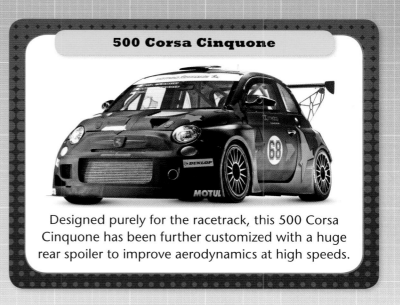

Designed purely for the racetrack, this 500 Corsa Cinquone has been further customized with a huge rear spoiler to improve aerodynamics at high speeds.

Above Romeo Ferraris have used a metal catalytic converter, better ECU and a stronger turbine that has increased the power of the 1.4-liter 4V turbo engine to a staggering 300 hp.

Honda CR-Z

Bisimoto Engineering took a Honda CR–Z and worked their **magic** to create a **thrilling** vehicle. The standard 1.5-liter four-cylinder engine has been rebuilt using Arias pistons, a Bisimoto valve train and a new **turbo**. These **modifications** have cranked the power all the way up to a mind-blowing 533 horsepower. The **dynamic** exterior is created with a custom **Gatorwrap** body wrap with colorful graphics. Bisimoto's CR-Z is so **awe-inspiring** that it is bound to turn heads wherever it goes.

Top speed **151** mph

0–60 mph **8.8** seconds

Power **533** horsepower

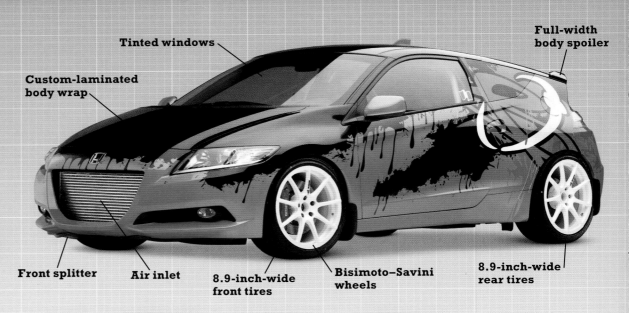

Tinted windows

Full-width body spoiler

Custom-laminated body wrap

Front splitter

Air inlet

8.9-inch-wide front tires

Bisimoto–Savini wheels

8.9-inch-wide rear tires

Below To increase the output of the 1.5-liter engine, Bisimoto have used an impressive Turbonetics billet turbocharger.

Measurements	
Length	160.6 in
Width	68.5 in
Height	54.9 in
Weight	2725 lb

Left The interior of this beefed-up Honda CR-Z has the feel of a race car thanks to the Buddy Club racing seats and six-point roll cage.

Ford — *Mustang GT*

When choosing a car to customize, one of the **all-time** favorites is the Ford **Mustang**. Design-World, a German tuning and customizing company, has improved the **performance** of the Mustang's powerful 5.0-liter V8 engine with a new air filter, air box and an **optimized** ECU. The exterior of the black Mustang is **customized** with impressive foil finishes, a new **grille**, diffuser and bumpers with skirts. The exterior is treated to some superb foil films in **metallic** orange, white and black.

Right The Mustang includes subtle orange highlights throughout the interior of the car, which coordinate with the exterior.

Measurements	
Length	188.5 in
Width	74.9 in
Height	55.8 in
Weight	7976 lb

Above A stylish aluminum gear shifter controls the six-speed transmission and allows the driver to enjoy the engine's high power ranges.

Rear spoiler

Metallic foil films

Mustang emblem

11.2-inch-wide rear tires

10-inch-wide front tires

Front splitter

Top speed limited **155** mph

0–60 mph **4.5** seconds

Power **435** horsepower

Renault
Clio 200 Cup

Car foiling company Cam Shaft have **transformed** the Clio 200 Cup into a **mean-looking** racing machine. The upgrades include a sports air filter and new **exhaust** system with dual end pipes for increased power and sound. The car's **suspension** has also been fine tuned. The most eye-catching customization is the dramatic **foil-wrapped** exterior. The car is covered in **orange** foil with a black top section featuring a number of manufacturer's logos dripping down the **bodywork**.

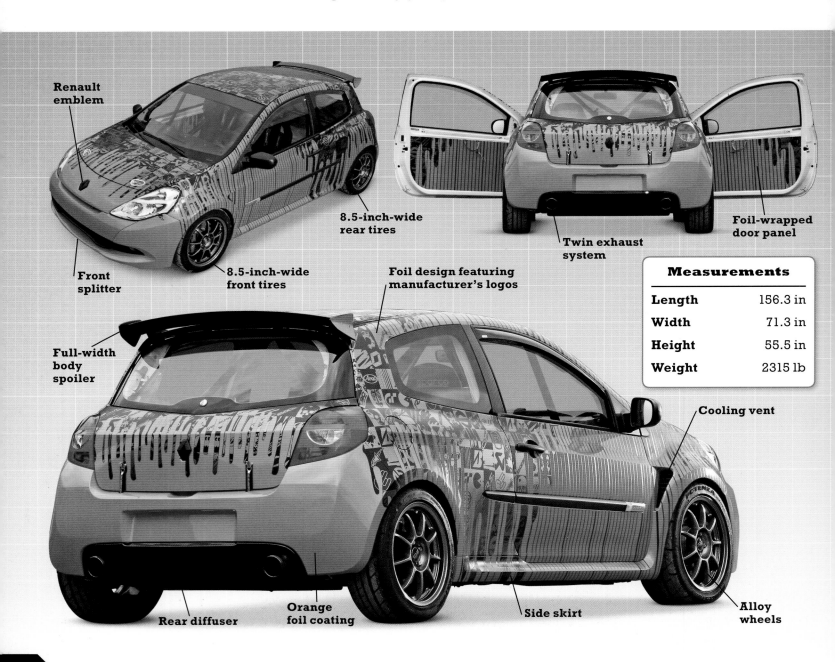

Renault emblem

Front splitter

8.5-inch-wide front tires

8.5-inch-wide rear tires

Twin exhaust system

Foil-wrapped door panel

Foil design featuring manufacturer's logos

Full-width body spoiler

Rear diffuser

Orange foil coating

Side skirt

Cooling vent

Alloy wheels

Measurements	
Length	156.3 in
Width	71.3 in
Height	55.5 in
Weight	2315 lb

Top speed **143** mph

0–60 mph **6.6** seconds

Power **200** horsepower

Renault Clio RS AS Ringtool

Cam Shaft have customized the Clio RS AS Ringtool with matte-graphite metallic foil on the surface, bright-green highlights and matching green wheel rims.

Above The foil is also featured in the interior of the car to give this super hatch a dynamic and urban look both inside and out.

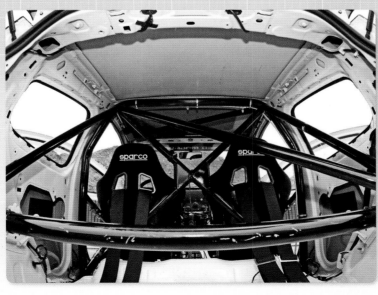

Right The interior of the car has been gutted to save weight. Some motor sports modifications such as a roll cage have been added.

Above The stock wheels were replaced in the Clio 200 Cup tuning program with lighter OZ Alleggerita HTL rims with a black finish.

Bentley *Continental GT3*

The engineers at Bentley have customized, tweaked and **modified** a Continental GT and created a **monstrously** powerful GT3 race car. They have removed over 2200 lb of weight and **reconfigured** the 4.0-liter V8 engine to produce 600 hp. The **striking** exterior features an aerodynamic body that helps to **maximize** downforce with optimized drag. The **custom** braking system has ventilated iron discs combined with four-piston calipers on the rear and **six-piston** calipers on the front.

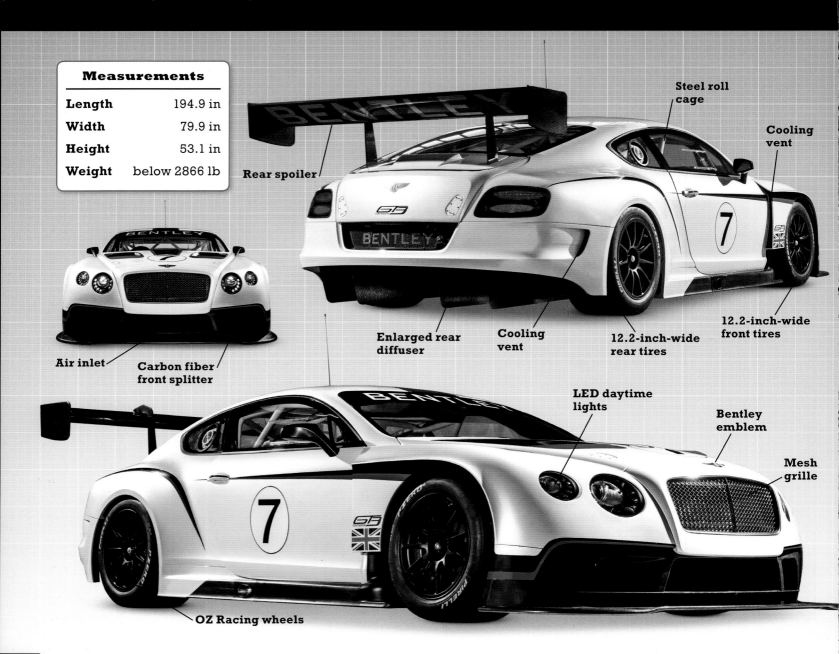

Measurements	
Length	194.9 in
Width	79.9 in
Height	53.1 in
Weight	below 2866 lb

Rear spoiler

Steel roll cage

Cooling vent

Enlarged rear diffuser

Cooling vent

12.2-inch-wide rear tires

12.2-inch-wide front tires

Air inlet

Carbon fiber front splitter

LED daytime lights

Bentley emblem

Mesh grille

OZ Racing wheels

Top speed	**170** mph
0–60 mph	**3.6** seconds
Power	**600** horsepower

Right The center console is made from lightweight carbon fiber and, like the side fascia and tread plates, it bears the GT3 emblem.

Below Despite the race specification, the GT3 remains a handcrafted Bentley, with upholstery hand-trimmed and stitched.

GT3-R

The GT3–R is a luxury performance car inspired by Bentley's Continental GT3 race car. Bentley are producing just 300 models of this limited edition.

Below Bentley's powerful but efficient 4.0-liter twin-turbo V8 engine provides the GT3 with highly competitive power in a compact and lightweight package that's perfect for racing.

Scion *Five Axis Widebody tC*

Five Axis took a Scion tC and gave it an **extreme** customization, turning this exciting car into a **visual** and audio extravaganza. Open the hatchback and an enormous 43-inch Pioneer **plasma** TV folds out of the trunk. To accompany this there are three **subwoofers**, four pairs of speakers in the doors and five **amplifiers**. To give this impressive car a unique look, Five Axis created an aggressive-looking **aerodynamic** body kit and coated the **bodywork** with a dramatic lime pearl paint.

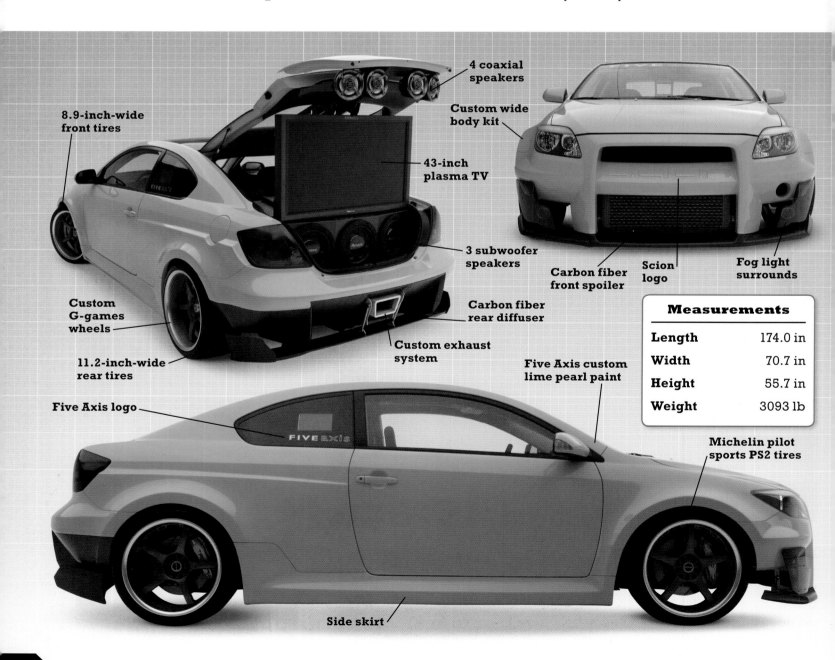

8.9-inch-wide front tires

4 coaxial speakers

Custom wide body kit

43-inch plasma TV

3 subwoofer speakers

Carbon fiber front spoiler

Scion logo

Fog light surrounds

Custom G-games wheels

Carbon fiber rear diffuser

11.2-inch-wide rear tires

Custom exhaust system

Five Axis custom lime pearl paint

Five Axis logo

Michelin pilot sports PS2 tires

Side skirt

Measurements	
Length	174.0 in
Width	70.7 in
Height	55.7 in
Weight	3093 lb

Top speed **127** mph

0–60 mph **6.8** seconds

Power **230** horsepower

Design by Alias

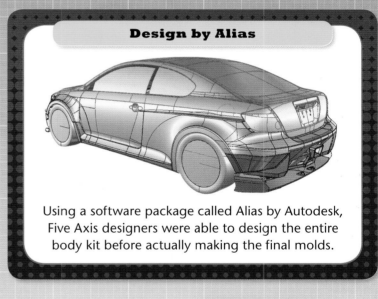

Using a software package called Alias by Autodesk, Five Axis designers were able to design the entire body kit before actually making the final molds.

Right In order to increase the output of this spectacular car a specially developed turbo system was added to the 2.4-liter engine.

Above The interior of this Scion tC features suede seats, Ultrasuede EcoDesign styling accents and specially designed upholstery.

Right The Formula 1 inspired front end includes high-performance fog lights with futuristic surrounds to increase the aerodynamics.

Ferrari 599 GTB Fiorano

Mansory, a specialist in **customizing** luxury sports cars, has modified and enhanced the **Ferrari** 599 GTB Fiorano to create the Mansory Stallone. The car boasts **high-performance** compressors and a custom-made intercooling system. **Modifications** to the body include a **carbon fiber** kit with new side skirts, a front spoiler and integrated rear diffuser. To accommodate the increased performance, **lightweight** forged **turbine-wheel** alloys have been installed by Mansory.

Above The outstanding 6.0-liter V12 engine has high quality components newly developed by the Mansory technicians.

Left Only the most exquisite materials have been used for the interior of this luxury car. The leather is hand-stitched by traditional craftsmen.

Measurements

Length	183.7 in
Width	77.2 in
Height	52.6 in
Weight	3721 lb

Top speed **211** mph

0–60 mph **3.6** seconds

Power **720** horsepower

Tinted windows

Carbon fiber bodywork

Air inlet

Bi-xenon headlights

12.8-inch-wide rear tires

Side splitter

10.8-inch-wide front tires

Front splitter

Porsche  997 GT2 RS

Edo Competition have customized the **Porsche** 997 GT2 RS to create one of the most **eye-catching** cars around. The engine has upgraded components, including new cylinder heads, **turbochargers** and a modified fuel system with three fuel pumps. The aerodynamic **body kit** includes **customized** front skirt, widened fenders and a Litronic headlight kit. A **performance** exhaust system has been installed that helps to **increase** the torque and give this mean machine a deep growl.

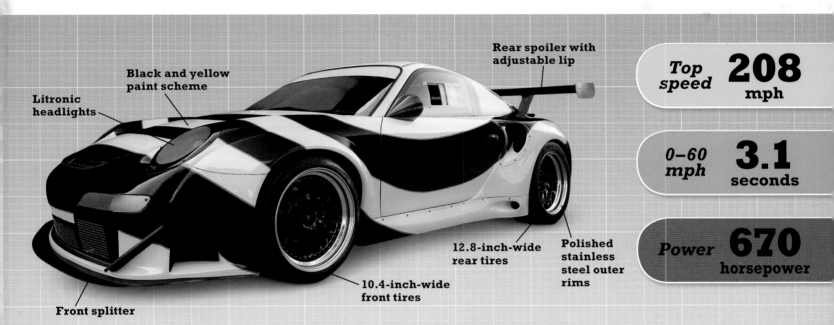

Rear spoiler with adjustable lip

Black and yellow paint scheme

Litronic headlights

Front splitter

10.4-inch-wide front tires

12.8-inch-wide rear tires

Polished stainless steel outer rims

Top speed **208** mph

0–60 mph **3.1** seconds

Power **670** horsepower

Measurements	
Length	92.9 in
Width	72.8 in
Height	52.2 in
Weight	3197 lb

Below The aerodynamic conversion kit includes a large rear spoiler made of ultralight carbon fiber for increased downforce.

Right The interior has been stripped of all luxuries and now has Recaro sports seats, a six-point harness and a sports steering wheel.

Glossary

Acceleration A measurement of the change in speed of a moving car.

Aerodynamics The science of designing smooth-shaped vehicles that travel faster and use less energy.

Air filter A device that removes and stops particles, such as dust, pollen, mold and bacteria, from entering the engine's cylinders.

Air inlets Openings that allow air into the engine area, which is used for the cooling systems.

Alcantara A high-tech and flame-resistant material.

Aluminum A silver-white metal often used on cars because of its lightweight properties.

Body kit A collection of exterior modifications for a car that changes its appearance and/or performance.

Brake calipers Devices that apply pressure to both sides of the brake disc to slow the car down.

Brushed chrome Chrome with the added effect of "brushed" lines on the surface giving it a textured finish.

Bumper The front or rear part of a car that has been designed to absorb impact in a collision.

Catalytic converter A device that converts toxic emissions in exhaust gas into less harmful gasses.

Carbon fiber A high-tech material used in car manufacturing because it is extremely strong and lightweight.

Chassis The main framework of a car that gives it strength, and to which other parts are fixed.

Cooling vent A vent that allows warm air to pass from the car into the atmosphere.

Diffuser A shaped section of the car's underbody that improves aerodynamics.

Downforce A force produced by airflow, which pushes downward, keeping the vehicle on the road.

Exhaust A system of pipes that are used to carry the burned and unburned gases from the engine into the atmosphere.

Grille A cover for the radiator that allows air to cool the engine.

Gull-wing doors Roof-hinged doors that open upward.

hp (horsepower) Measurement of the amount of power a car engine can produce.

Intercooler An apparatus for cooling gas inside a supercharged engine.

LED (Light Emitting Diode) A device used for digital displays in the instrument panel and for headlights in place of standard bulbs because of its durability and brightness.

mph (miles per hour) The measurement of speed that shows the distance covered in one hour.

Piston A metal disc that slides up and down inside an engine cylinder.

Roll cage A specially engineered framework of reinforcements to protect the passenger cabin of a car.

Scissor doors Car doors that rotate upward on a hinge, rather than outward as with most cars.

Shifter The device used to change the gears of a vehicle. Also commonly called a gear stick.

Side skirts A panel that runs between the front and rear wheel arches. It can be modified to change the appearance of the car.

Splitter A device integrated into the underbody of a car that redirects airflow, increasing aerodynamics and downforce.

Spoiler A wing-shaped device attached to a car that improves aerodynamics.

Supercharger A device for supplying air under high pressure to the cylinders of an engine.

Suspension A system of components attached to the wheels of a car to make the ride feel smoother and more comfortable.

Titanium A silvery-gray metal with high corrosion resistance. It is strong, lightweight and very expensive.

Turbo (or turbocharger) A device for increasing power that uses hot gases to drive a pump, forcing more air into the engine cylinders.

Xenon A gas that is used in some high-performance cars' headlights to give dramatically improved vision.